POTATOES

The lowly tuber, in any of its various forms, is one of our most delicious vegetables. Here are wonderful recipes for virtually every kind of potato, from Idaho to new, from sweet potatoes to yams. The classic baked, buttered, mashed and scalloped recipes are included, but so, too, are a wide variety of innovative dishes such as "Potato and Zucchini Torta" (an appetizer), "Potato Soufflé" (an exotic main dish) and "Dorset Potato and Jam Tarts" (a marvelous dessert). Here, too, are plenty of flavorful salads and unique potato accompaniments.

secrets of vegetable cooking

. . . is a series of attractive, low-priced cookbooks, each concerned with a specific vegetable and, most important, each containing a collection of more than 50 distinctive and delicious recipes for the broadest range of vegetable dishes. A special treat—the soup to nuts of vegetable cookery.

Inez M. Krech, author of the entire series, is well known as a writer (she was the co-author of "Naturally Italian") and as the editor of more than 200 cookbooks. She lives in New Jersey.

secrets of vegetable cooking

Inquiries should be addressed to
Crown Publishers, Inc., One Park Avenue, New York, New York 10016

Printed in the United States of America

Published simultaneously in
Canada by General Publishing Company Limited

Library of Congress Cataloging in Publication Data

Krech, Inez M.
   Potatoes.

   (Secrets of vegetable cooking)
   1. Cookery (Potatoes) I. Title. II. Series: Krech,
Inez M. Secrets of vegetable cooking.
TX803.P8K66 1981   641.6'521   81-7838
ISBN 0-517-54445-8   AACR2

10 9 8 7 6 5 4 3 2 1
First edition

DESIGN AND COVER PHOTOGRAPH BY ALBERT SQUILLACE

POTATOES

by inez m. krech

primavera books ❧ crown publishers, inc. / new york

Introduction

All schoolchildren know two things about Sir Walter Ralegh: he threw his splendid cloak in the mud so that the great Queen Elizabeth should not soil her feet, and he carried the first potato to England. The second story at least is myth. In 1577 Sir Francis Drake received potatoes from Indians off the coast of Chile, and Ralegh obtained the tubers from some of Drake's crew (or, according to some historians, he found the tubers in some Spanish vessel he pillaged during the years he was flourishing as a privateer). Sir Walter introduced the potato into Ireland on his own estates near Youghal. By 1710 they were grown so extensively that white potatoes became known as "Irish potatoes." In Ecuador, white potatoes were called papas, and the sweet potato was a batata, but the second name was adopted for all kinds.

Potatoes were described and illustrated in John Gerard's Herbal, published in London in 1597. In spite of this early recognition of them, centuries were to pass before they became generally popular. The cultivation of potatoes, both white and sweet, was developed in the highlands of the West Coast of South America, especially in the areas now known as Ecuador, Peru and Chile, but tubers of wild potatoes were used in North America by the Hopi and Navajo, also in central Mexico. North of the isthmus potatoes were an incidental food (corn, beans and squash were far more important), while in the South American highlands they were a major staple, since the altitude made other vegetable crops too difficult to grow. The tubers and blossoms were sculptured on pottery, indicating their significance as a cult object as well as food. Also, then as well as now, alcoholic beverages were made from potatoes.

Potato starch, industrial alcohol, dehydrated potatoes, potato flour, and various animal foods are prepared from the potato.

The retail shopper has no idea of the species of potatoes he buys; if lucky, one finds them identified by season. Winter potatoes: January through March. Spring potatoes: April through June. Early summer: June through August. Late summer: August through September. Fall potatoes: after October 1. Potatoes are grown in every state of the U.S.A.

Three quarters of the annual crop is stored and marketed in winter and spring. Idaho and Maine potatoes make up the bulk of the fall crop. They are mealy and dry, good for baking and mashing. There are also waxy fall potatoes, good for salad. New potatoes are harvested before maturing so the skin is thin.

When shopping, look for firm, smooth potatoes with no cuts or bruises. The greenish coloration sometimes seen results from exposure to light, either in growing or in storage. The green part of the potatoes can taste somewhat bitter, but one would need to eat enormous amounts of it for it to be harmful. It is hard to predict the cooking quality of a potato from its appearance; if in doubt consult your produce grocer.

Store potatoes in the dark, in a dry, well-ventilated place; at 45°F. to 50°F. potatoes will keep for several months; at 70° to 80°F. they should be used within a week. When potatoes are stored below 40°F., some of the starch turns to sugar, which spoils the flavor. Potatoes stored for a long time begin to shrink, and sprouting starts.

Growing potatoes in the home garden is most rewarding, but it does require space and considerable effort. Potatoes are subject to a number of pests, including the fungus that caused the Irish potato blight of 1845-1846. But potatoes that are dug by hand are without blemishes; today commercial white potatoes are dug by machine and many are nicked or bruised. (An experienced potato digger can grub out 75 barrels of potatoes a day, but a machine digger can grub out 1500 barrels a day.) In the home garden, it is possible to dig a few new potatoes in August, leaving the balance to grow larger. These early "marbles" are delicious.

Many years ago, in the Penn-Dutch market in Lancaster, I saw a tiny booth selling what looked like bunches of green leaves, of a pretty shape and delicate green. I couldn't resist this, so stopped to inquire. They were sweet potatoes; and this is how sweets are propagated, by shoots from seed potatoes, which are then planted out in rows. I bought a large bunch and so had my first experience of growing them. I have had good sweets often, but never as delicious as those, which I harvested just before Thanksgiving. That set a standard hard for any commercial sweet to match.

There are rather dry firm sweets, with a pale yellow flesh, and a closely related tuber that is so pale it is called a "white sweet potato." More popular is the sugary orange-fleshed tuber mistakenly called a yam. There are other species grown in South America, even some with all white or purple flesh, but these are not grown commercially. The familiar kinds are grown in about half of the States.

All kinds of sweets are far more perishable than white potatoes. They can be kept for a few weeks only, and refrigeration is harmful to them. When purchasing them, avoid any with spots or bruises, as they will not keep. Because of their delicate texture, sweet potatoes are not machine dug; even a small nick would start spoilage. At home, if soft spots or spoilage appear, discard the potato; the flavor of the whole potato will be affected.

Do you think the potato is costly? To be sure, it costs more today than it used to, but of this price over 75 percent is for transportation and the expenses of the various middlemen. And with all that, it remains a bargain when compared with other vegetables.

A white potato weighing 100 grams (3-1/2 ounces) provides about 75 calories, not a lot considering the valuable nutritional content: amino acids, B vitamins, good supply of potassium. Potatoes are low in sodium. The vitamin C content varies with age—new potatoes have about 26 milligrams per 100 grams while potatoes stored 6 months have about a third of that. A single potato can provide a quarter of the daily requirement of vitamin C.

A sweet potato weighing 100 grams provides about 115 calories. It is also a good source of amino acids and potassium, but is an unusually good source of vitamin A. The orange-fleshed tubers can provide as much as 10,000 international units; the pale dry tubers provide about 600 international units.

For best food value, cook potatoes in their skins and do not overcook. If you need to peel them, remove the thinnest possible layer of peel. Potatoes can be prepared in a pressure cooker, but they tend to break up under pressure, so this is not the preferred method. The liquid used for cooking white potatoes can be used for soup or stock; it contains water-soluble nutrients leached out in cooking.

Mature potatoes, which have been in storage, generally labeled "winter potatoes," should be started in cold water; when they reach the boiling point, they should be simmered. The reason for this is that these potatoes have a mealy dry texture packed with starch grains; the starch expands in the heat of cooking and the potato tends to crumble when boiled instead of simmered. New, or immature, potatoes, with their more compact texture, should be started in boiling water so that they are cooked through to the center.

The potato is our most popular vegetable, and no wonder since its delicious flavor and nutritional value make it adaptable to so many preparations, even desserts. Since the white potato keeps so well in storage, it is a convenience food all by itself. No need to use canned or frozen potatoes except in emergencies; canned potatoes are very soft, frozen potatoes are crumbly. When preparing dishes such as stews for freezing, leave out the potatoes; they can be added later and will have better texture.

A Note to Cooks

Some of the recipes call for the use of a blender or food processor. If you lack these appliances, do not discard the recipes. Any food can be sliced, chopped or minced with a chef's knife on a chopping board. A mortar and pestle can be used for grating, and there are inexpensive hand-operated utensils for shredding. The best tool for puréeing is the hand-operated food mill, available in several sizes.

Unsalted butter and olive oil were used in testing recipes. If it matters to the recipe, the ingredient list will specify "unsalted butter"; otherwise use what you prefer, but remember to adjust salt. If butter is prohibited, use margarine instead. Any vegetable oil or polyunsaturated oil can be substituted for olive, but the taste will be slightly different.

All recipes use relatively low amounts of salt and very little sugar; if you prefer more or less, adjust to taste. If either is prohibited, simply omit. You may want to adjust flavor with a little lemon juice or an additional pinch of an herb if salt is omitted. If fructose is permitted, use that in place of cane sugar.

■   Ingredients are listed in **bold** type when they are first mentioned in the instructions and thereafter whenever it seems helpful in following the directions.

Baked White Potatoes

1. Any size of potato and any kind of potato can be baked. However, best results can be expected with larger potatoes and with potatoes designated as "baking potatoes." It doesn't matter if they were raised in Idaho, Maine, Long Island, or where.

2. Choose **potatoes** of 6 to 8 ounces. (Oddly enough, 4-ounce potatoes seem to need the same amount of time.) Count 1 potato per serving. Scrub them with a stiff brush. Remove any damaged areas or large eyes (sometimes tough fibers surround these). If you are using russet potatoes, which are covered with a russet "bloom," you may wish to scrape this off. Brush again and rinse. Let potatoes dry.

3. For crisp browned skin, pour a teaspoon of **olive** or **vegetable oil** in the palm of one hand and roll the potatoes, one at a time, in the oil.

4. Potatoes can be baked at any temperature, which makes them adaptable to varied oven uses, but the ideal temperature is 400°F. Preheat the oven before you start.

5. Bake the potatoes for 30 minutes, then turn them over and pierce the side now uppermost with a steel fork or skewer. Bake for 20 to 30 minutes longer, until potatoes are done to your taste.

6. Remove potatoes from oven, make a cut across and down the center of each one, and press gently to spread open. Add a **cube of butter.**

7. Finished potatoes may be sprinkled with salt and pepper, or paprika. They can be served with sour cream and chives, with grated cheese, or with other garnishes, but they are most delicious plain.

8. Never wrap potatoes with foil for oven baking; that's only good when cooking them on a barbecue grill. Foil makes it impossible for you to see if they are cooking properly; it keeps the skins from becoming crisp, in fact they tend to become leathery; all the steam is retained in the foil wrapping and the potatoes become soggy. Worst of all, foil retains heat a long time and that makes it possible for public eating places to serve potatoes baked hours before, even days before, which have lost all their good taste. The argument that foil helps retain vitamin C would be more impressive if potatoes were our only source of this vitamin. Just do your best for the vitamin content by serving as soon as baked. For good uses of foil, see later recipes.

Baked Sweet Potatoes

1. Choose perfect **sweets,** whether dry or moist, without soft or damaged spots. (Sweets with spoiled areas should be discarded as the taste will be affected all through.) Scrub them.

2. Bake in a preheated 400°F. oven (or adjust temperature to other dishes). After 40 minutes, turn potatoes over and pierce the side uppermost with a skewer or steel fork. If you are baking the moist sweet potatoes (or yams), the sugary syrup will start to seep out through the hole you have made as the potato reaches the right stage of doneness. You may want to put a sheet of foil on the bottom of the oven to catch these drips.

3. A sweet potato of 6 to 8 ounces will be fully baked in 50 minutes to 1 hour. Don't bake longer or the outer portion will become hard. A potato of 12 to 16 ounces will require 1-1/2 hours and should be turned more than once for even cooking.

4. The skin of sweets is not eaten; it is leathery. Serve them in the skin; each person scoops out the flesh on his own plate. Or peel and use for the other recipes. Baked sweets are more delicious—sweeter and juicier—than potatoes boiled or steamed. Nevertheless, either method can be used if you have less time and do not want to light the oven.

Baked Stuffed Potatoes

preparation time: 15 minutes
cooking time: 1-1/4 hours
serves 6

6 baking potatoes, each about 8 ounces
3 scallions
2 ounces butter
6 tablespoons dairy sour cream
2 egg yolks
salt and pepper
paprika

1. Scrub **potatoes,** and bake them following the basic recipe (see Index).
2. Wash and trim **scallions;** keep about 1 inch of the green leaves (the rest can be saved for soup or salad). Cut scallions across into thin round slices. Heat the **butter** in a small skillet and sauté scallions until tender. Set aside.
3. Beat **sour cream** and **egg yolks** together.
4. When potatoes are baked, cut them lengthwise into halves, and scoop out the pulp without damaging the shells. Use a potato masher to mash the pulp, then mix in the scallions and butter. When butter is melted and absorbed, beat in the sour cream and egg yolks. Season with **salt** and **pepper** to taste.
5. Pile the filling into the shells, heaping it up in the center. Sprinkle with **paprika.**
6. Return to the oven, still at 400°F., and bake for 10 to 15 minutes, until golden brown on the top. Serve 2 halves to each person.

Baked Stuffed Potatoes à la Maryland

preparation time: 25 minutes
cooking time: 1-1/4 hours
serves 6

6 baking potatoes, each about 8 ounces
2 cups cooked fresh crab meat
6 ounces fresh mushrooms
2 ounces butter
3 ounces sliced blanched almonds
1/2 cup heavy cream
salt
dash of Tabasco
1/4 cup chopped parsley

1. Scrub **potatoes,** and bake them following the basic recipe (see Index).
2. Pick over **crab meat** and discard any cartilage. Wipe **mushrooms** with a damp cloth and remove a slice from the stem end. Separate stems and caps; chop stems, slice caps.
3. Melt **butter** in a skillet and sauté sliced **almonds** for 2 minutes, stirring all the while. Lift out almonds to a plate, leaving the butter in the pan.
4. Add **mushroom stems** to the skillet and sauté for 2 minutes. Add **caps** and continue to cook for 5 minutes longer. Gently fold in **crab meat** and set aside.
5. When potatoes are baked, cut them lengthwise into halves, and scoop out the pulp without damaging the shells. Put pulp in a bowl, mash it, then mix in the mushroom and crab mixture and any butter remaining in the pan. Add the **cream** and mix. Season with **salt** to taste and add **Tabasco** and **parsley.**
6. Spoon the mixture into potato shells, mounding it up a little in the center. Divide the **almonds** among the potato halves, sprinkling about 1/2 tablespoon on each half.
7. Return potatoes to the oven, still at 400°F., and bake for 10 to 15 minutes, until almonds are browned. Serve 2 halves to each person as a main course for lunch or supper.

Foil-Wrapped Potatoes for Barbecue

preparation time: 10 minutes
cooking time: 1 to 1-1/2 hours
serves 6

6 baking potatoes, about 6 ounces each
6 pieces of heavy-duty foil, 12 × 24 inches
oil

1. Scrub **potatoes** as for baking, removing any damaged areas. Do not dry them.

2. Fold each piece of **foil** into a square and brush the center of each one with a few drops of **oil.** Put the still damp potatoes on the foil squares, and close the wrapping in drug-store fashion, or pull up the 4 corners as if wrapping an apple dumpling, and twist together, closing the sides well.

3. Place the packages on the barbecue grill, or in the ashes at the edge of the fire if your grill is large enough. Use tongs to turn them at least 3 times. The exact time for cooking depends on your fire. Test them by squeezing gently; if the package feels soft, potatoes are done.

variations: If you are cooking on an open fire in a fire pit, bury the potatoes in the ashes at the edge of the pit. For this kind of cooking, it is also practical to wrap potatoes in mud with a lot of clay in it, or in wet newspapers, or even in wet corn husks.

New potatoes can be wrapped in a single sheet of foil; the outside of the potatoes will char slightly; they are delicious this way.

Braised Potatoes

preparation time: 5 minutes
cooking time: about 20
        minutes
serves 6

1-1/2 pounds potatoes
2 tablespoons olive oil
1 cup chicken stock, hot
1-1/2 ounces Parmesan cheese
3 tablespoons minced parsley

1. Wash and peel **potatoes,** and cut into cubes of about 1 inch.
2. Heat **olive oil** in a 10-inch skillet with a tight-fitting cover. Add **potato cubes** and cook over moderate heat, stirring often, until potatoes are golden on all sides, about 10 minutes.
3. Add **chicken stock,** reduce heat, cover, and let potatoes braise for about 5 minutes. Test potatoes; they should be tender.
4. Grate the **cheese** and mix it with **parsley.** Sprinkle it evenly over the potatoes, cover, and leave over low heat for 2 minutes, until cheese is melted. Stir, then serve. Great with hamburgers or chops.

Potatoes Braised in Foil

preparation time: 5 minutes
cooking time: 50 minutes
serves 6

2 pounds potatoes, about 6
6 pieces of heavy-duty foil, 12 × 24 inches
3 ounces butter
salt and pepper
3 shallots
1 teaspoon dried rosemary or marjoram

1. Wash and peel **potatoes.** Cut them into thin slices and divide into 6 portions. Preheat oven to 350°F.
2. Fold each piece of **foil** into a square and divide the **butter** among them. Add **1 portion of potato** and sprinkle with **salt** and **pepper.** Peel and mince **shallots** and divide among the potatoes. Finally, crush the **herb** in a mortar and sprinkle on top.
3. Fold up the packages in drug-store fashion. Bake for about 50 minutes. These can be baked at higher or lower temperature to adjust to other dishes in the oven.

French-Fried Potatoes (Pommes Frites)

preparation time: 10 minutes
cooking time: about 8 minutes
per batch
serves 6

2 pounds baking potatoes
vegetable oil or shortening
salt

1. Wash and peel **potatoes.** Cut each one into an even rectangle; the cut-off portions should be covered with cold water and refrigerated. Cut each rectangle into pieces square in cross-section, about 1/2 inch, and as long as the rectangle.
2. Wash pieces in cold water and roll in paper towels until dry. (If you prefer, they can be soaked, but it is not necessary.)
3. Heat **oil** or **shortening** to 375°F. in a deep-fryer with a thermostat; or use a wok or frying kettle and test the fat with a frying thermometer. Line a baking sheet with paper towels and preheat oven to 250°F.
4. Dip the frying basket into the oil, then lift it out and add some of the **potatoes.** Fry potatoes until golden brown and done to your taste. Let one piece cool and test to be sure. Transfer cooked potatoes to the baking sheet and keep hot until all are done.
5. Let the oil return to 375°F. and continue cooking potatoes in batches until all are done. Sprinkle with **salt** and serve in a basket or bowl lined with paper napkins.

The chief problem with French Fries is getting the center cooked before the outside fries too hard. Potatoes of the same species can vary according to harvesting time, so it is not easy to estimate the timing. Here is a second method for frying, which takes away a lot of the guesswork.

1. Prepare the **potatoes** as in Steps 1 and 2.
2. Heat the **oil** or **shortening** to 370°F., and cook potatoes in batches for about 7 minutes. Transfer them to the paper-lined baking sheet and let them rest.
3. Just before serving, reheat the frying kettle to 380°F., and fry the **potatoes** again, only about 10 pieces at a time, for about 8 minutes longer, until crisp and golden. Sprinkle them with **salt** and serve without delay.
4. Let the **oil** cool, then pour slowly through a filter into a clean container. When completely cold, store in a glass bottle with airtight closure and refrigerate.

note: If you cut potatoes with the French fry slicer of a food processor, you will have smaller pieces, about 3/8 inch across, and they will be slightly curved. They may need a minute or so less cooking.
See variations that follow.

Matchstick Potatoes (Pommes Allumettes)

1. Cut **potatoes** into 1/4-inch sticks, half the size of the usual French fries.
2. Fry following the basic recipe, but for only 4 to 5 minutes.

Pont-Neuf Potatoes (Pommes Pont-Neuf)

1. Cut **potatoes** into 3/4-inch sticks, larger than the usual French fries, like stubby little logs.
2. Fry following the basic recipe, but use the second method, and for the first frying keep the **oil** or **shortening** at 350°F. Fry **potatoes** for 10 to 12 minutes the first time, for about 3 minutes for the second.

Chips (British Fries)

1. Cut **potatoes** into 1/2-inch sticks, as in the basic recipe.
2. Use **rendered beef suet** (from around the beef kidneys) or **lard** (rendered pork fat). Fry following the basic recipe, using whichever method you prefer.
3. Sprinkle finished chips with **malt vinegar** and **salt.**

Chips (American Style)

These are called "crisps" or "game chips" in Britain; in America they are sometimes called Saratoga chips from the place where they are said to have been invented.

1. Peel **potatoes,** cut off the small ends (store in cold water), and cut the remaining ovals into the thinnest slices you can manage, ideally 1/16 inch. Drop them into cold water until all are sliced.
2. Heat **oil** or **shortening** to 375°F. as in the basic recipe. Drain potatoes and roll in towels to dry completely.
3. Fry a handful at a time for 2 or 3 minutes, turning them to brown on both sides. Drain on paper towels. Do not salt them until ready to serve.
4. Serve as a garnish for poultry and game, especially pheasant. They will never be as dry and crisp as commercial chips, so they are not practical to serve with dips. If there are any left, they make a crunchy snack by themselves.

Death Valley Potatoes

preparation time: 5 minutes
cooking time: 30 to 40 minutes
serves 6

2 pounds potatoes
4 cups lard
coarse salt

1. Scrub **potatoes** thoroughly; do not peel. Cut them lengthwise into quarters. If they are very large potatoes, cut each quarter again into halves. Roll in paper towels to dry thoroughly.

2. Heat the **lard** in a deep-fryer to 375°F. You may not need 4 cups; use enough to make the fryer about two-thirds full. While the lard heats, line a baking sheet with paper towels and heat oven to 250°F.

3. Put one quarter or one third of the **potato pieces** in the fryer basket and gently lower into the fat. They should be able to move freely without sticking together; move them with a fork if necessary. Fry for 8 minutes, then lift out one piece and test. If not tender, continue to fry. If tender, lift out the basket and dump potatoes onto the baking sheet. Keep warm in the oven until all are finished. Continue to fry the potatoes, a batch at a time, until all are cooked. Be sure **lard** returns to 375°F. between batches.

4. Pat **potatoes** with more paper towels to remove excess fat. Sprinkle with **coarse salt,** and serve in a basket lined with paper towels.

variations: Instead of lard, you may use vegetable oil, although the taste of the potatoes will be different.
If you lack a French fryer with thermostat, potatoes can be fried in a wok, which requires less fat or oil, or in a frying kettle. Test the temperature with a frying thermometer.

Hashed Brown Potatoes

preparation time: 10 minutes
cooking time: 15 minutes, plus
20 minutes to boil
potatoes
serves 6

2 pounds potatoes
1/4 to 1/2 cup bacon fat
salt and pepper
6 tablespoons chopped scallion tops
3 tablespoons chopped parsley

Serve this dish for breakfast. After cooking the breakfast bacon, save the fat for cooking the hashed browns.

1. Cook the **potatoes** the day before you make this dish. Scrub potatoes, cover with cold water, and cook at a simmer for 15 to 20 minutes, until potatoes are tender but not mushy. Drain, cool, then refrigerate without peeling.

2. Peel cold **potatoes** and dice them. Heat enough of the **fat** in a large skillet to have a layer about 1/4 inch deep. Add the potatoes and press into a mass. Sauté over moderate heat until the bottom is brown and crusty.

3. Use a pancake turner to flip the **potatoes** over. It does not matter if they break up or crumble. Season the browned side with **salt** and **pepper.** Continue to cook until brown and crusty on the second side.

4. Flip over again. Season the second side with salt and pepper. Cut into wedges to serve. Sprinkle each serving with 1 tablespoon **scallion tops** and 1/2 tablespoon **parsley.**

Sautéed Whole New Potatoes

preparation time: 5 minutes
cooking time: 25 minutes
serves 6

1-1/2 pounds small new potatoes
6 tablespoons clarified butter
coarse salt
chopped parsley

Choose potatoes all of the same size and have ready a heavy skillet large enough to hold them all in a single layer.

1. Use a vegetable peeler to peel **potatoes,** taking off the thinnest possible layer.
2. Heat **butter** in the skillet, add **potatoes,** and cover the pan. Cook over low heat, gently shaking the pan now and then, for about 12 minutes.
3. Uncover pan and turn **potatoes** over, using wooden spoons to turn them. Cover again and cook for about 10 minutes longer, until potatoes are tender.
4. Sprinkle with **coarse salt** and **parsley** and serve with meat or fish.

variations: Cook potatoes in oil instead of butter. Just before they are done, add a mixture of minced parsley and shallots.
Cook potatoes in goose fat instead of butter.

Sautéed Cut-up Potatoes

preparation time: 15 to 20
minutes
cooking time: 15 to 20 minutes
serves 6 to 8

2 pounds large potatoes
1/2 cup clarified butter
salt

1. NOISETTE POTATOES: Wash and peel the **potatoes.** Use the large end of a melon-ball scoop to cut as many balls from the potatoes as possible. Put the rest of the potatoes in a bowl, cover with cold water, cover the bowl, and refrigerate for other uses. (See Raw-Potato Salad.) **Follow with Steps 4 and 5.**

2. CHÂTEAU POTATOES: Wash and peel the **potatoes.** Cut them into quarters and trim each quarter to the shape of a plum or large olive. Cover the trimmed pieces with water and refrigerate as in Step 1. **Follow with Steps 4 and 5.**

3. PARISIENNE POTATOES: Cut **potatoes** as for noisette potatoes, and prepare **3 tablespoons meat glaze** and an equal amount of chopped fresh **parsley.**

4. Heat **clarified butter** in a heavy skillet. Add **potatoes** and sauté over low heat until golden on the bottom. Shake the pan to prevent sticking. After 10 to 12 minutes, turn pieces over with wooden spoons and continue sautéing until tender. Test with a skewer.

5. Sprinkle noisette or château potatoes with **salt.** Spoon **meat glaze** over Parisienne potatoes and shake to coat all the pieces. Sprinkle in the **parsley.** Serve without delay.

Potato and Leek Soup (Soupe Bonne Femme)

preparation time: 15 to 20
minutes
cooking time: about 1 hour
serves 6

1 onion, 4 ounces
1 pound leeks
1 tablespoon olive oil
2 ounces butter
1 pound potatoes
1 teaspoon salt
dash of white pepper
1/2 teaspoon saffron threads
4 cups boiling water
2 cups milk

This is a simple country soup, easy to make, delicious and nourishing. The vegetables are still in chunks, in contrast to the variations that follow.

1. Peel and chop the **onion.** Trim the **leeks;** cut off all but 1 inch of the green leaves; put them aside for stock making. Wash leeks thoroughly. Cut across into 1/2-inch slices, then wash again. Cut slices into 1/4-inch dice.
2. Heat **oil** and **butter** in a soup kettle and dump in **onion** and **leeks,** with whatever water clings to leeks. Cover the kettle and let the vegetables cook gently until translucent. Do not let the vegetables brown at all, and stir now and then with a wooden spoon or paddle.
3. Peel **potatoes** and cut into 1/4-inch dice. Add to the soup kettle and stir to mix. When potatoes have simmered for 2 minutes, sprinkle in the **salt, pepper** and the **saffron,** which has been crushed in a mortar. (Saffron is not in the classic French soup, but this addition gives a golden touch to the soup, an improvement over the pale color of the vegetables.)
4. Pour in the **water,** bring again to a boil, then reduce to a simmer and cook for 30 to 40 minutes, until potatoes are tender enough to mash with a spoon.
5. Pour in the **milk,** bring to a boil, then remove soup from heat. Serve in a tureen, or ladle into deep soup plates.

Crème Vichyssoise

1. Make Potato and Leek Soup (preceding recipe), but omit the saffron. At the end of Step 4 turn the soup, part at a time, into a food mill or blender, and purée it. Return purée to the soup kettle.
2. Instead of milk, pour in **2 cups light cream** and bring the soup almost to the boiling point.
3. Garnish with a mixture of **chopped parsley** and **snipped chives.**

Crème Vichyssoise Glacée

This is the cold version of the simple French soup, invented by Louis Diat when he was chef at the New York Ritz-Carlton.

1. Make Crème Vichyssoise (preceding recipe). Cool the soup after Step 2, stirring it often to prevent formation of a skin on top.
2. Strain the cooled soup through a fine sieve, and stir in **1 cup cold heavy cream.** Chill the soup.
3. Ladle into bouillon cups or cream soup bowls and sprinkle with **snipped chives,** about 1/2 teaspoon per serving. The chilled soup will make 8 servings.

Potato and Celery Soup

preparation time: 15 minutes
cooking time: 30 to 40 minutes
serves 8

1 pound celery
4 to 6 parsley sprigs
2 pounds winter potatoes
2 quarts water
1 teaspoon salt
1/2 cup dairy sour cream
1/2 cup heavy sweet cream

1. Divide **celery** into 3 portions: the coarse outer ribs and outer leaves; the tender inner ribs; all the tender yellow leaves from inner ribs. Wash and drain all portions. Wash **parsley.** Pat dry celery leaves and parsley, chop together, and set aside for garnish. Cut tender inner ribs into crosswise slices no thicker than 1/8 inch; there should be at least 1 cup of the slices. Drop the slices into a saucepan, cover with boiling water, and cook for 2 minutes. Drain, rinse with cold water, and drain again. Set aside. Cut the outer ribs into large chunks and drop them and the outer leaves into a deep soup kettle.
2. Scrub and peel **potatoes,** cut into chunks, and add to **celery.** Pour in the **water** and add the **salt.** Bring to a simmer and cook for about 20 minutes, until the potatoes will break when touched with a fork.
3. Lift out and discard the celery pieces. Put the **potatoes** and **liquid** through a food mill into another soup pot. Add the blanched **celery slices** to the purée and set the kettle over low heat. Stir often so the purée does not stick to the pot. When soup is at a simmer, remove from heat.
4. Mix both **creams** in a bowl, stir in a ladle of the hot soup to heat the creams, then mix into the balance of the soup. Transfer soup to a tureen, or serve into cream soup bowls, and sprinkle mixed **celery** and **parsley leaves** over the top.

variations: To make a more nutritious soup, use unsalted chicken stock in place of water, or use half stock and half water.
To make a thicker soup, beat 2 egg yolks with the mixture of creams before adding to the soup.
To make a simpler and cheaper soup, omit the mixture of creams. The plain soup is a good dish for convalescents.

Steam-Baked Potatoes

preparation time: 5 to 10 minutes
cooking time: 40 to 50 minutes
serves 4

2 tablespoons olive or vegetable oil
3 large potatoes, each about 8 ounces
sea salt crystals
2 ounces unsalted butter
1/4 cup minced fresh parsley, or a mixture of parsley and coriander leaves

1. Spoon the **oil** into an 8-cup casserole with a cover and set it in a warm place so that the oil can be swirled around to coat the bottom. Preheat oven to 350°F.

2. Scrub and peel the **potatoes.** Cut them into quarters. With a paring knife round off all the square edges so that you finally have pieces with the size and shape of a blue prune-plum. Put all the cut-off scraps in a plastic bowl, cover with water, and refrigerate; they can be used for soup or salad.

3. Put the shaped **potatoes** in the casserole and roll them around to coat them with a thin film of **oil.** Pour in 1 tablespoon **water** for each potato piece—for this batch that will be 3/4 cup water. Sprinkle a few tiny pinches of **sea salt crystals** on the potatoes.

4. Cover the casserole and bake for 20 minutes. Uncover, and with wooden spoons or paddles turn the potatoes over. If the water has all evaporated, add a little more, about 1 teaspoon per piece. Cover again and continue baking until done to your taste. Most of the water and oil should be absorbed and the potatoes should have a pale golden crust.

5. Melt the **butter** and pour into a serving bowl. Lift **potatoes** into the bowl, turn them around to coat with butter, and sprinkle with the **minced herb.** Serve at once, or cover the bowl if there is a delay.

variation: This method also works well for new potatoes. Peel them and leave them whole. They may need a few minutes longer to become tender. This method is adaptable to any number of servings, from one to dozens, but works best if the potatoes are in a single layer in the casserole. If you are preparing a large number, you may need to increase the oil.
Another variable is the oven temperature. These taste just as delicious baked at a lower temperature for a longer time or at a higher temperature for a shorter time, so you can adjust to other dishes being baked at the same time.

Steamed New Potatoes (Pommes à la Vapeur)

preparation time: 5 minutes
cooking time: 20 minutes
serves 6

18 new potatoes, each about 2 ounces

This method works with any kind of potato, but for appearance and taste try to choose Red Bliss, with rosy skins. Select them all the same size for even cooking. These are delicious plain, but they can be garnished with chopped parsley or sauced with melted butter.

1. Scrub Red Bliss **potatoes** with a brush. If you have potatoes with very thin skin, do not use a brush, but rub them gently with a rough cloth. With a vegetable peeler or lemon zester, cut off a narrow strip around the middle of each potato; do not peel them otherwise.

2. Put enough water in a vegetable steamer or saucepan to reach just below the rack or basket. Bring the water to a boil and adjust heat so that steam escapes through the rack. Add the **potatoes,** in a single layer if possible, and cover the pot. Let them steam for about 20 minutes. (If potatoes are not in a single layer, turn them after 10 minutes to bring the bottom layer to the top.) Test with a skewer. Steam for a few more minutes if necessary.

3. Lift out the rack or basket and turn potatoes into a serving dish lined with a cloth towel. Serve at once.

Mashed Potatoes

preparation time: 10 minutes
cooking time: 20 minutes
serves 6

1-1/2 pounds winter potatoes
1 teaspoon salt
1-1/2 ounces butter
1/4 cup milk or light cream, hot

The best mashed potatoes are those freshly made and mashed by hand using a "beetle" (a wooden pestle) or potato masher. For best flavor and tenderness, do not use an electric mixer, a blender or a food processor, as these develop too much gluten and make the potatoes tough.

1. Wash and peel **potatoes,** cut into even-size pieces, and cover with cold water. Add **salt.** Bring to a boil, then simmer for 15 to 20 minutes, until tender.
2. Drain off the water, but leave potatoes in the saucepan and set it on an asbestos pad over low heat. Add the **butter,** cut into bits. Mash potatoes, mixing in the butter as you go.
3. Just before serving, add as much of the **milk** or **cream** as you need to give the right texture—fluffy and tender, but not soupy. Serve at once.

note: If you are cooking potatoes in advance to use for potato cakes or boxty, just mash them and add half of the listed amount of butter. Add no milk or cream. Let potatoes cool to room temperature before storing in refrigerator. One pound of potatoes will give you about 2 cups mashed.

Duchess Potatoes

preparation time: 20 minutes
cooking time: 20 minutes, plus
time for glazing or
browning
serves 8, more as garnish

2 pounds potatoes
1 teaspoon salt
2 ounces butter
white pepper
3 whole eggs, or 2 whole eggs and 2 egg yolks

1. Wash and peel **potatoes,** cut into even-size pieces, and cover with cold water. Add **salt.** Bring to a boil, then simmer for 15 to 20 minutes, until tender.

2. Drain off the water and put **potatoes** through a food mill or ricer. Return to the saucepan and add the **butter.** Set the pan over very low heat or on an asbestos pad and beat in the butter while drying the purée. Season with **white pepper** to taste, and a little more **salt** if needed.

3. Beat whole **eggs,** or **eggs and yolks,** and add to the potatoes. Use a wire whisk to make the mixture fluffy.

4. Spoon potatoes around planked foods, or around coquilles or individual baking dishes. Or spoon into mushrooms or hollowed-out tomatoes or other vegetables, to be arranged around serving platters for garnish. For even fancier garnishing, spoon potatoes into a large pastry bag and pipe it around, using a large metal tip. You can make small rosettes, leaf shapes, rings, braids, etc.

5. Since these potatoes are already cooked, they need only glazing in oven or broiler, so they are added to planks or coquilles only when the rest of the food is almost done. Leaves, rings, braids, etc., can be browned on a baking sheet and added at serving time.

Potato and Parsnip Purée

preparation time: 10 to 15 minutes
cooking time: 30 minutes
serves 6 to 8

1 pound parsnips
salt
2 ounces butter
1 tablespoon honey
2 pounds potatoes
2 plum tomatoes (optional)
white pepper

1. Scrub and trim **parsnips,** but do not peel them. Split them lengthwise, and cut into chunks.

2. Put chunks into a saucepan, add cold water to reach the top of the pieces, add 1/2 teaspoon **salt,** and bring to a steady gentle boil. Cook for 8 to 10 minutes, until parsnips are very tender.

3. Lift **parsnips** into a food mill. Pour off and reserve remaining cooking liquid. Purée parsnips into a mixing bowl. Add 1 ounce of the **butter** and the **honey,** and mix. Cover the bowl loosely and set it in a warm place or in a hot-water bath.

4. Clean the food mill; you will need it for the potatoes.

5. Scrub **potatoes** and remove any damaged spots; do not peel. Cut them into even-size chunks.

6. Put chunks in a large saucepan, add cold water to reach the top of the pieces, add 1 teaspoon **salt,** and bring to a steady gentle boil. Cook for 15 to 20 minutes, until potatoes are on the verge of falling apart.

7. While the potatoes cook, blanch and peel the **tomatoes.** Remove hard portion at stem end and split tomatoes. Press out seeds and juice and cut the flesh into 1/4-inch cubes. Set aside for garnish.

8. Lift **potatoes** into the food mill, part at a time if your mill does not hold them all. Pour off and reserve remaining cooking liquid. Purée potatoes into the mixing bowl containing the **parsnips.** Add remaining **butter.**

9. Mix the vegetables together until butter is melted, then slowly add enough of the reserved cooking liquids to give the purée the texture you prefer. Adjust the **salt** if necessary, and add **white pepper** to taste. Beat with a wooden spoon until purée is fluffy.

10. Spoon purée into a round serving bowl and sprinkle **tomato cubes** around the edge. Serve at once.

Colcannon

preparation time: 15 minutes
cooking time: 30 minutes
serves 6 to 8

1-1/2 pounds winter potatoes
salt
1-1/2 pounds kale
6 ounces leeks
1 cup milk
2 ounces butter
pepper

This Irish dish was traditionally eaten at Hallowe'en, but it is an excellent winter dish. Frequently, cabbage is used instead of kale with equally good results.

1. Wash and peel **potatoes,** and cut into chunks. Cover with cold water, add 1/2 teaspoon **salt,** and bring to a boil. Simmer for 20 minutes, until potatoes are tender.

2. While potatoes cook, wash **kale** thoroughly and pull off all thick stems and any damaged leaves. Put kale in a heavy saucepan, add 1 cup water and a pinch of **salt,** and cover the saucepan. Bring to a boil and cook for 10 to 12 minutes, until kale is tender.

3. While potatoes and kale are cooking, wash **leeks,** cut into slices, including green tops, and wash again. Put leeks in a heavy saucepan, add **milk,** and simmer until leeks are tender.

4. Drain **potatoes,** drop in the **butter,** and mash until tender. Drain **kale** and chop in the colander, or turn out onto a chopping board and chop. Set aside to drain further.

5. Lift out **leeks.** Pour the **milk** through a sieve lined with a moistened muslin. (This step is important as leeks may release some additional grit during cooking.) Drop leeks into mashed potatoes, and mash further, until leeks are mixed into potatoes.

6. Beat chopped drained **kale** into the potatoes until mixture is pale green. Add as much of the strained **milk** as needed to give a texture you like. Colcannon should be fluffy. Season with **salt** and **pepper** to taste.

7. In Ireland the completed mixture is piled into a deep serving dish, a well is made in the center, and melted butter is poured into the well. The melted butter is used for a sauce. Good with lamb and beef.

variations: In Scotland carrots are added to the mashed potatoes. In Ireland as well as in Germany certain symbols, like the Twelfth-Night Cake symbols, were mixed into the colcannon. They usually included a coin (penny or sixpence), a ring, a thimble, and a button, meaning money, marriage, the status of spinster or bachelor, and poverty to the person who found the symbol in his or her portion.

Champ

preparation time: 10 minutes
cooking time: 20 minutes
serves 6

1-1/2 pounds winter potatoes
salt
16 scallions, no thicker than a pencil
1 cup milk
2 ounces butter
white pepper

A popular recipe from Northern Ireland, it is traditionally eaten on Fridays.

1. Wash and peel **potatoes,** and cut into chunks. Cover with cold water, add 1/2 teaspoon **salt,** and bring to a boil. Simmer for 20 minutes, until potatoes are tender.
2. Wash and trim **scallions.** Remove root ends and ragged tops, and use the rest of the green tops. Chop scallions to small pieces, and cover with the **milk.** Simmer gently until very tender.
3. Drain **potatoes,** mash them, and beat in the **butter.** Mix in the cooked **scallions,** and add as much of the **milk** reserved from cooking the scallions as needed to give good texture. Season with more **salt** if needed and **white pepper** to taste.

variation: Instead of scallions, use 1 cup of snipped chives, blanched for 1 minute.
This dish is also called "stelk" and "chappit tatties."

Potato Kugel (Jewish Potato Pudding)

preparation time: 35 minutes
if grating by hand
cooking time: 1 hour
serves 4 to 6

2 pounds potatoes
1 large onion, about 5 ounces
2 eggs
2 tablespoons flour or matzo meal
4 tablespoons rendered chicken fat
1/2 teaspoon salt
1/2 teaspoon baking powder (optional)

Chicken fat is traditional in kugel and it gives the best flavor. If this is forbidden because of the cholesterol, substitute polyunsaturated oil.

1. Wash and peel **potatoes.** Grate them, and put the pieces in a muslin bag or a triple layer of cheesecloth. Squeeze the bag or cheesecloth to extract as much liquid as possible. Turn potato pulp into a mixing bowl.
2. Peel **onion** and grate into the potatoes. Beat the **eggs** and add, along with the **flour,** 3 tablespoons of the **fat,** the **salt** and **baking powder.** Mix well. Preheat oven to 375°F.
3. Grease a shallow baking pan, about 6-cup size, with remaining fat. Spoon in the potato batter.
4. Bake the kugel for 1 hour, until browned on top and bottom.

variation: To speed up the preparation, cut potatoes into 1-inch pieces and grate in a food processor fitted with the steel blade. Grate the onion in the same way. Preparation time will be reduced to 20 minutes.

Ecuadorian Potato Cakes (Llapingachos)

preparation time: 15 minutes
cooking time: 35 minutes
serves 4 as main course, 8 as
first course or
accompaniment

1-1/2 pounds potatoes
8 ounces yellow onions
1-1/2 ounces butter
1 tablespoon vegetable oil
salt and pepper
6 ounces Edam, Tilsit or Munster cheese
5 tablespoons lard
2 tablespoons annatto seeds

1. Wash and peel **potatoes** and cut into small pieces. Cover with water, bring to a boil, and simmer for about 20 minutes, until tender.

2. Peel and chop **onions.** Melt **butter** in a skillet, add **oil,** and sauté onions until golden and soft, not browned. If the pan seems too dry, cover the skillet and finish cooking by steaming.

3. Drain and mash **potatoes** and beat in the **onions** and any butter and oil remaining in the pan. Season with **salt** and **pepper.** Divide the mixture into 8 portions of equal size.

4. Meanwhile, chop or shred the **cheese,** and divide into 8 portions. Shape each portion of potatoes into a flattened pattie, and make a hole in the middle. Put 1 portion of cheese into the hole and pat potatoes around cheese to enclose it completely.

5. Melt the **lard** in a saucepan and add **annatto seeds.** Sauté over moderate heat until lard is orangey-red, about 1 minute. Pour lard through a sieve and discard seeds.

6. Heat part of the **annatto oil** in a heavy saucepan. Sauté the llapingachos, part at a time, on both sides until well browned; the cheese in the center should be melted. Add more oil to cook the rest of the cakes.

7. Serve with fried fish, or fried plantains, or sliced avocados and tomatoes and other vegetables. Use as a first course or main course; these make a good supper dish.

Irish Potato Cakes

preparation time: 10 minutes
cooking time: 30 minutes
serves 4 to 6

1 pound potatoes
1 ounce unsalted butter
1 teaspoon salt
1/2 teaspoon caraway seeds
1/3 to 1/2 cup unbleached flour
1/4 cup vegetable oil or melted butter for sautéing

These cakes are served for breakfast in Ireland, or with "a nice fry"—a high tea or supper dish that includes bacon, lamb kidneys, eggs, halved small tomatoes, all fried. They make a good accompaniment to fried or baked fish and cold roast beef.

1. Wash and peel **potatoes,** and cut into quarters. Cover with water and bring to a simmer. Cook for about 20 minutes, until potatoes are tender enough to break up when pierced with a fork.
2. While potatoes cook, cut the **butter** into bits and drop into a mixing bowl.
3. Put drained **potatoes** through a food mill into the bowl with the butter. Add the **salt,** and mix with a wooden spoon until butter is melted and mixed into potatoes. (Do not beat, just mix.) Let potatoes cool to room temperature.
4. Crush **caraway seeds** in a mortar and sprinkle over potatoes. Add 1/3 cup **flour** and only as much of the rest as needed until the potatoes form a mixture that leaves the sides of the bowl. Use the smallest amount of flour possible to avoid "doughy" cakes.
5. Pat out the mixture and level to 1/2-inch thickness. Cut out 2-inch rounds. Pat remaining mixture into a smooth layer, and continue to cut out rounds until all is used. You will have about 14 rounds.
6. Heat half of the **oil** or **butter** and sauté half of the cakes on one side for 5 minutes. Turn over and brown on the second side for 5 minutes longer. Keep hot in a low oven until all are done. Heat remaining oil or butter and sauté the rest of the cakes.

variation: If you are using the oven for another dish, you can bake these instead of sautéing them. Place on a buttered baking sheet in a 350°F. oven and bake on one side for 15 minutes, then turn and bake for 15 minutes longer; the cakes will puff up but will remain paler than when sautéed.

Alvin Kerr's Rösti (Swiss Shredded Potato Cake)

preparation time: 15 to 20 minutes, plus time to chill potatoes
cooking time: 30 to 40 minutes
serves 4

2 pounds boiling potatoes
salt
1 ounce butter
1 ounce hydrogenated white vegetable shortening

1. Scrub **potatoes** thoroughly; do not peel them. Cover with 4 cups water, or enough to cover them, and add 2 teaspoons **salt.** Bring water quickly to the boil and simmer potatoes for exactly 15 minutes, no longer. They will be partly cooked. Drain them, cool, and chill, still unpeeled, for several hours or overnight.

2. Peel the chilled **potatoes** and shred them on the shredding side of a grater. Do not cut them! Do not chop them! Do not slice them! Do not grate them! Only shred them.

3. Melt **butter** and **shortening** in a heavy 8- to 9-inch skillet. Add potatoes and cook over moderate heat for 2 minutes. Sprinkle with **salt** to taste. With a pancake turner press top and sides gently to form a cake.

4. Continue cooking until the underside is well browned and crusty. Place a buttered plate on top and turn skillet and plate over together. Slide the cake back into the skillet, browned side up, and continue cooking until cake is brown and crusty on the second side.

5. Slide the cake onto a warmed serving plate. Cut into wedges to serve.

Potatoes in Cream Sauce

preparation time: 10 minutes
cooking time: about 25
    minutes
serves 6

1-1/2 pounds small potatoes
2 ounces butter
1/2 cup heavy sweet cream
salt and pepper

This dish is called "O'Riley" in Irish cookbooks, "à la crème" in French cookbooks, and "creamed" elsewhere. it can be varied to suit all sorts of tastes, and is an excellent way to prepare potatoes in advance.

1. Wash the **potatoes** and cook in water to cover for about 12 minutes; they should be about half cooked. Let them cool, and peel them. This much can be done in advance.

2. Melt the **butter** in the top pan of a double boiler set over barely steaming water. Add the peeled **potatoes** and pour in the **cream.**

3. Cover the pan and let potatoes steep in the cream until it is almost absorbed. Stir with a wooden spoon once or twice. If potatoes are done and cream absorbed before you are ready to serve, leave the top pan over hot water, but remove the lower pan from the heat. When ready to serve, season to taste.

variations: To give this a Hungarian flavor, add paprika, a mixture of sweet and hot to taste. To give it a German flavor, add caraway seeds. To make a prettier dish, add 1 cup fresh green peas, blanched, just before serving; you may need a little more cream with the peas.

Potatoes and Apples

preparation time: 12 minutes
cooking time: 20 minutes
serves 8

2 pounds potatoes
2 cups water
1 teaspoon salt
1 pound mellow cooking apples
2 to 4 teaspoons sugar
1 tablespoon lemon juice

This famous German dish is often called Himmel und Erde (heaven and earth), but in my grandmother's vegetarian cookbook, published in 1898, it is called simply "potatoes with apples." A country dish, it is the perfect companion to all sorts of sausages, but also tastes great with baked ham and game birds.

1. Wash and peel **potatoes,** cut into cubes, and put in a large saucepan with the **water** and **salt.** Bring to a boil and cook at a simmer for 10 minutes.
2. Peel the **apples,** cut into quarters, and remove the pits. Add apples to the potatoes and continue to simmer until both are very tender. The water should be almost all absorbed. Add more, a few tablespoons at a time, if it cooks away before potatoes are done.
3. Mash the mixture, or put through a food mill; either way it is delicious. Add **sugar** and **lemon juice** and mix well.

variations: If the apples are tart, you may not need any lemon juice. If you plan to put the mixture through the food mill, you can cook apples with both pits and peels for more flavor.
Flavor the purée with cinnamon, nutmeg or mace, or allspice if you like. Add 2 ounces butter and mix in until melted.
For a splendid garnish, chop 5 bacon strips and 2 onions, about 5 ounces, into small pieces. Sauté them together until golden brown—the bacon should be crisp—and sprinkle over the top of the purée.

Potato Gratin with Red Pepper

preparation time: 20 minutes
cooking time: 1 hour
serves 6

1 red bell pepper, 6 to 8 ounces
1 onion, 4 ounces
1 tablespoon oil
1 ounce butter
1-1/2 pounds potatoes
6 ounces whole-milk mozzarella cheese, shredded

This gratin is a fine accompaniment to meat dishes; for vegetarians it makes an excellent main course.

1. Wash the **red pepper;** with a vegetable peeler remove the skin. (Or cut into quarters and broil, skin side toward the heat source, until charred. Then peel off the skin.) Discard stem, ribs and seeds, and cut the pepper into pieces—squares or strips; the size and shape can be random, but try to make them all about the same.
2. Peel and chop the **onion.** (Or chop in a food processor fitted with the steel blade.)
3. Heat the **oil** and half of the **butter** in a small skillet and sauté the **onion** over low heat until golden.
4. Use remaining **butter** to coat a 6-cup casserole, which can be shallow like a lasagna dish, or deep, and the inside of the cover, or a sheet of foil.
5. Wash and peel **potatoes.** Cut them to fit the tube of a food processor. Insert the slicing disk and slice the potatoes. (Or slice by hand, making 1/8-inch slices.) Preheat oven to 350°F.
6. In the buttered casserole, arrange first a layer of **potato slices,** then a scattering of **sautéed onion** and **red pepper pieces.** Sprinkle with some of the **shredded cheese.** Continue layering until all ingredients are used, ending with potatoes and cheese. In a shallow casserole, you can make 2 layers; in a deeper casserole, make 3 or 4 layers.
7. Cover the casserole with buttered cover or foil sheet. Bake in the oven for about 1 hour, until potatoes test done. The top should be golden. Serve from the casserole.

variations: For a zippier flavor, use "pizza cheese," a mixture of mozzarella, Parmesan and Romano.
All potatoes are different. This recipe usually requires no additional liquid, but if your potatoes are dry-textured, you may need to add a little unsalted stock or water. Test after 15 minutes of baking, and add the liquid, 1/4 cup at a time.

Potato Gratin with Mushrooms

preparation time: 40 minutes
cooking time: 1 to 1-1/2 hours
serves 8

1-1/2 ounces dried cèpes or porcini
1 pound fresh mushrooms
1 onion, 4 ounces
1 garlic clove
2 ounces butter
2 pounds potatoes
2 ounces Gruyère cheese
2 ounces Parmesan cheese
1/4 cup chopped parsley
1 cup light cream
salt and pepper

1. Rinse the dried **cèpes,** then soak them in water to cover for 30 minutes. Trim the fresh **mushrooms,** wipe with a damp cloth (or wash if they are very dirty), and let them dry. Peel and chop the **onion,** and peel the **garlic.**

2. Lift **cèpes** from the soaking water. Remove and discard stems (they are tough). Filter the soaking liquid through a muslin, and reserve. Remove stems from fresh **mushrooms** and chop them. Slice the caps of both fresh and dried mushrooms. Use just a little of the **butter** to coat an 8-cup gratin dish.

3. Melt remaining **butter** in a large skillet. Sauté the **onion** and chopped **mushroom stems** until onions are golden and translucent. Add sliced **mushroom caps** and sauté for 5 minutes, stirring. Put **garlic** through a press into the mixture.

4. Pour off the liquid released by **mushrooms** and add the filtered soaking liquid from **dried mushrooms.** Set aside. Preheat oven to 350°F.

5. Peel **potatoes** and slice by hand, or trim to fit a processor tube and cut with the slicing disk, making thin slices.

6. Arrange a thin layer of **potatoes** in the buttered dish. Cover with half of the **mushrooms** and **onions.** Grate both **cheeses** and mix together. Sprinkle one third of the cheese over the mushroom layer, then add half of the **parsley.** Add more potatoes, then the rest of the mushrooms and onions. Add another third of the cheese and the rest of the parsley. Finish with the last of the potatoes and the last of the cheese.

7. Mix the **mushroom liquids** and **cream,** and season with **salt** and **pepper** to taste. Carefully pour the mixture into the dish, lifting the potatoes if necessary to let the liquid reach the bottom. Bake for 1 to 1-1/2 hours. If the top starts to brown too much, reduce oven temperature. Serve with a plain roast meat or poultry, or as a separate course with a green salad.

Betty Lou's Scalloped Potatoes

preparation time: 20 minutes
cooking time: 1-1/4 hours
serves 8

2 pounds potatoes
3/4 pound yellow onions
3/4 pound Cheddar cheese
3 ounces unsalted butter
salt and pepper
3 cups milk, approximately

1. Peel **potatoes** and cut into thin slices, using a chef's knife, or the slicing disk in a food processor. Peel and slice **onions.** Shred or grate the **cheese.**
2. Use 1 tablespoon of the **butter** to coat a 2-quart casserole with a cover. Butter the inside of the cover also. Preheat oven to 350°F.
3. Layer the **potatoes, onions** and **cheese** in the buttered casserole, sprinkling each potato layer with a little **salt** and **pepper** and dotting it with some of the **butter.** Finish with a potato layer, dotted with the rest of the butter. Pour in **milk** to reach halfway to the top. Cover the casserole.
4. Bake in the preheated oven for 1-1/4 hours, or until potatoes are done to your taste. The milk should be almost all absorbed.
5. If you like the top brown, uncover the casserole for the last few minutes and let it brown to your taste.
6. Serve from the casserole to accompany chicken or veal, or as a main dish for a vegetarian meal.

Potatoes and Cabbage à la Chinoise

preparation time: 10 minutes
cooking time: 20 minutes
serves 6

1-1/2 pounds potatoes
salt
1-1/2 pounds Chinese celery cabbage (napa)
1 onion, 3 ounces
1 ounce gingerroot
2 tablespoons peanut oil
2 tablespoons soy sauce

1. Wash and peel **potatoes,** and cut into 1/4-inch sticks. (If you have a food processor, cut potatoes to fit the tube; use the French-fry slicer, or julienne blade, and process potatoes.) Put potato sticks in a saucepan, cover with boiling water, and add 1/2 teaspoon **salt.** Bring again to a boil and cook for 10 minutes; the pieces should still be crunchy. Drain.
2. Wash the **cabbage,** drain, then slice across into thin shreds. Put in a saucepan, sprinkle with 1/2 teaspoon **salt,** and cover with boiling water. Let stand for 5 minutes, then drain, rinse with cold water, and drain again.
3. Peel and mince **onion** and **gingerroot.**
4. Heat **oil** in a wok, and add **onion.** Sauté, stirring, until onion is translucent. Add **gingerroot** and cook for 1 minute. Add **potato sticks,** and stir-fry for 3 minutes. Finally, stir in the **cabbage** and stir-fry until potato and cabbage are tender.
5. Pour in the **soy sauce,** mix everything, and cook for 2 minutes longer. An excellent accompaniment to pork.

Sweet-Potato Stew

preparation time: 25 minutes
cooking time: 40 minutes
serves 6 to 8

3 pounds dry sweet potatoes, about 6
1 pound small yellow onions, about 8
1-1/2 pounds tomatoes
2 green bell peppers
butter
salt and pepper
few drops of Tabasco
beurre manié (optional)

Do not use the orange-colored sweet potatoes called yams for this stew. The best potato is the so-called "white sweet potato" which has a dry texture and pale color, but regular sweet potatoes will do.

1. Peel **potatoes** and cut on the diagonal into 1/2-inch slices. Peel **onions** and cut each into halves from stem to blossom end; leave enough of the root in place to keep the halves from falling apart. Blanch the **tomatoes,** peel them, and chop. Roast or broil the **peppers** until the skin is blackened, then peel them and discard stems, ribs and seeds. Cut peppers into shreds or diamonds.

2. Butter a heavy stewpot or top-of-stove casserole, and also butter a sheet of foil large enough to cover it. Layer the **vegetables** in the pot, in random order, sprinkling each layer with a little **salt** and **pepper.** Pour in 1 cup of **water,** or more if needed to have about 1 inch in the bottom. Add **Tabasco.**

3. Place the sheet of foil, buttered side down, on the vegetables and make a few holes in it for steam to escape. Cover the pot. Cook over moderate heat for 30 to 40 minutes, until potatoes are tender. Or bake in a 350°F. oven for 1-1/4 hours.

4. If there is a lot of liquid in the pot, thicken it with **beurre manié** (a mixture of butter and flour kneaded together), crumbling it in a tiny bit at a time. This is an excellent vegetarian main dish, also a fine accompaniment to poultry or pork.

Potato and Zucchini Torta

preparation time: 15 minutes
cooking time: about 30
minutes
serves 4 to 6

1 pound small new potatoes
1 pound zucchini
1 garlic clove, halved
1 tablespoon butter
2 tablespoons olive oil
2 ounces pecorino Romano cheese
4 eggs
4 ripe plum tomatoes
1/4 cup chopped parsley

1. Scrub **potatoes;** do not peel them. Cover with boiling water, bring again to a boil, and cook for 10 minutes. Drain, rinse with cold water, peel, and dice.

2. Wash, scrape, and trim **zucchini.** Grate it or chop in a food processor. Rub a deep 9-inch pie or quiche dish with the **garlic** pieces; discard them. Butter the pan with the tablespoon of **butter.** Preheat oven to 375°F.

3. Heat the **oil** in a skillet and over low heat gently cook **potato dice** until they are pale gold. Add **zucchini** and cook and mix for 1 minute. Remove pan from heat. Grate the **cheese.**

4. Break the **eggs** into a mixing bowl and beat to mix. Add grated **cheese.** Use a slotted spoon to add **potatoes** and **zucchini** to the eggs. Leave the oil in the skillet.

5. Pour the mixture into the buttered pan. Bake in the preheated oven for 15 to 20 minutes, until eggs are baked and puffed up.

6. While the torta is baking, blanch and peel the **tomatoes,** dice them, and mix with **parsley.** Sauté the mixture in the oil remaining in the skillet until tomatoes are soft.

7. Cut the torta into wedges to serve, and garnish each serving with a spoonful of the tomato mixture. This can be served hot or cold.

Potato and Cheese Torta

preparation time: 10 minutes
cooking time: 45 minutes
serves 4 to 6

1-1/2 pounds potatoes, 4 or 5
2 ounces unsalted butter
4 ounces Fontina cheese
1/2 pound salami
1/4 cup chopped parsley
olive oil
chicken stock (optional)
2 ounces Parmesan cheese

1. Scrub **potatoes;** do not peel them. Cover with cold water and bring to a simmer. Cook for about 12 minutes.

2. Butter a 6-cup baking dish or deep pie dish. Cut the rest of the **butter** into small dots. Cut **Fontina cheese** into thin slivers. Remove any rind from **salami** and cut into small dice. Preheat oven to 375°F.

3. Peel **potatoes** and cut into thin slices. Make a layer of some potatoes in the buttered dish. Add some **cheese** slivers, some **salami** dice, some **parsley** and a few dots of **butter.** With a feather pastry brush, flick a few drops of **olive oil** all over. Continue layering, ending with potatoes; flick more drops of oil over the top. If the potatoes are very dry, add a few tablespoons of **chicken stock** with every layer.

4. Grate **Parmesan cheese** and sprinkle over the top. Bake in the oven for 30 minutes, or until potatoes are completely tender and the top golden.

5. Cut into wedges to serve. Garnish with sprigs of watercress and grilled tomato halves.

Potato Soufflé

preparation time: 30 minutes
cooking time: 1 hour
serves 8

1-1/2 pounds potatoes
4 ounces unsalted butter
1/2 pound mushrooms
3 ounces Parmesan cheese
salt and pepper
4 egg yolks
6 egg whites

1. Peel **potatoes,** cut into pieces, and simmer in water just to cover until very tender. Put potatoes through a food mill into a large mixing bowl. Beat in 2 ounces of the **butter.**

2. While potatoes cook, wipe **mushrooms** clean, trim the stems, and chop. Sauté them in 1-1/2 ounces of **butter** until tender. Stop cooking while there is still some mushroom juice in the pan.

3. Use remaining **butter** to coat the inside of an 8-cup soufflé dish. Grate the Parmesan **cheese.** Sprinkle about 1 tablespoon on the buttered surface, turning the dish around until well coated with cheese.

4. Mix the **mushrooms** and their cooking juices into the **potatoes,** then beat in remaining **cheese.** Taste, and add seasoning as needed. Preheat oven to 325°F.

5. Beat the **egg yolks,** one at a time, into the potatoes. Add a pinch of **salt** to **egg whites,** and beat with a whisk or rotary egg beater until stiff but not dry. Mix about a third of the egg whites into the potatoes, then gently fold in the rest.

6. Spoon the batter into the prepared dish, then push it toward the center. Bake in the preheated oven for 45 minutes.

7. Serve as a main dish at a vegetarian meal, or as an accompaniment to lamb or veal.

variations: When mushrooms are not available, onions make a delicious substitute.

Omit mushrooms or onions. Mix 1/2 cup heated milk into the potatoes as soon as the butter is mixed in. Cook 8 bacon slices until very crisp, drain well, and crumble. Mix crumbles into the potatoes just before adding egg yolks. (Not for vegetarians, but good!)

Snow Pudding

preparation time: 15 minutes
cooking time: 1 hour and 15
minutes
serves 6 as accompaniment,
4 as main course

1-1/2 pounds potatoes
1 large bay leaf
1 teaspoon butter
2 ounces Romano cheese
1 cup low-fat cottage cheese
1 cup half-and-half (cream and milk)
1 ounce blanched almonds, grated
1 teaspoon celery salt
4 egg whites
salt

This soufflé manqué was designed for people who are not able to eat egg yolks. Also it contains only 12 grams of fat per serving. The flavor is delicate. An excellent accompaniment to beef or lamb; or serve it as a vegetable main dish, accompanied by ratatouille or other colorful vegetables.

1. Wash and peel **potatoes,** and cut into 1-inch chunks. Put in a saucepan, add the **bay leaf,** and just cover with water. Bring to a boil and simmer for 12 to 15 minutes, until potatoes are very soft, but not falling apart. Discard bay leaf and pour off the water.
2. While potatoes cook, use the teaspoon of **butter** to coat the inside of a 6-cup soufflé dish. Grate the **Romano cheese,** and sprinkle some of it into the dish to coat the entire inside. Set the dish aside.
3. Set the saucepan of **potatoes** over very low heat (simmer flame), and shake the pan to dry potatoes a little. Then mash with a potato masher. Beat in **cottage cheese, half-and-half,** remaining **Romano cheese, almonds** and **celery salt.** The mixture should be smooth and fluffy. Set aside to cool. Preheat oven to 375°F.
4. Drop **egg whites** into a mixing bowl. Add a tiny pinch of **salt,** and beat with a rotary beater until stiff peaks stand up straight when beater is withdrawn. With a spatula, fold one third of the egg whites into the potatoes. Then more gently fold in the remainder.
5. Spoon the batter into the prepared dish. Bake in the oven for about 1 hour. The pudding will not puff as much as a soufflé. The sides and bottom will be golden brown and the top browned in spots when pudding is done. Serve promptly.

Spanish Potatoes

preparation time: 15 to 20 minutes
cooking time: 1 hour
serves 8

2 pounds potatoes
salt
2 eggs, lightly beaten
flour
1/2 cup olive oil
4 garlic cloves
8 ounces Spanish onions
1/2 teaspoon ground saffron
2 cups chicken stock or water
3 ounces blanched almonds
chopped parsley
oil-cured black olives

1. Peel **potatoes** and cut into 3/4-inch-thick slices. Sprinkle slices lightly with **salt,** then one by one dip them into beaten **eggs,** or brush potatoes with egg, and then coat with **flour.** To make this easy, spread flour on a sheet of wax paper and turn each slice onto it. Shake off excess flour.
2. Use a tiny amount of the **oil** to coat a 2-quart casserole. Heat the rest in a heavy skillet and sauté the **potato slices,** a few at a time, until golden; they will not be fully cooked in the center. Lay them in the casserole, overlapping them to make a fairly even layer.
3. Peel **garlic.** Peel and chop **onions.** Grind **saffron** in a mortar, then add it to the **chicken stock** or water.
4. Sauté the **garlic** in the oil remaining in the skillet. (Add more oil if needed.) When just golden, lift out the garlic to a plate. Sauté **onions** until tender, then add **almonds** and continue to cook until onion and almonds are golden.
5. Put sautéed **garlic, onions, almonds** and saffron-flavored **stock** in a blender or food processor and whirl until almonds are ground. Pour this over the potatoes, lifting them as needed to let liquid reach the bottom.
6. Cover the casserole and bake for 1 hour, or longer if you prefer. Serve from the casserole, with **parsley** sprinkled around the edge and a few **black olives** for garnish. Good with fish dishes.

variation: If you wish, you can cook this on top of the stove. Use low heat. Do not stir, but now and then shake the pan to prevent sticking. It is easier to do it in the oven, although not as authentic.
If you do not care for garlic, omit it. However, the garlic and the olive oil give it the characteristic taste.

Cornish Potato and Bacon Pie

preparation time: 15 minutes
cooking time: 45 to 60 minutes
serves 4 to 6

3/4 pound thick bacon (about 12 strips)
1 pound potatoes
1 onion, 3 ounces
3 eggs
3/4 cup milk
1/4 cup all-purpose flour
salt and pepper

1. Cut **bacon** strips into 1-inch pieces, put them in a cold skillet, and cook them over medium heat, stirring often to help even cooking. When the fat is translucent and the meat beginning to crisp, about half done, lift the pieces out to a thick layer of absorbent paper and let them drain.

2. Use 1 tablespoon of the **bacon dripping** to coat a square or rectangular baking pan, about 2-quart size; the exact shape is not important, but it should not be round. Preheat oven to 400°F.

3. Wash and peel **potatoes,** and shred them by hand or in a food processor. Peel and chop the **onion.**

4. Break **eggs** into a bowl, add the **milk,** and beat well. Mix in the shredded **potatoes,** chopped **onion,** and half-cooked **bacon** pieces. Stir in the **flour;** make sure it is well mixed in, not in lumps. Season with **salt** and **pepper** to taste. (The amount of salt depends on the saltiness of the bacon.)

5. Heat the greased pan in the oven until very hot, then pour in the batter. Bake for 45 minutes to 1 hour. The batter will puff up while baking, then fall when removed from the oven like a Yorkshire pudding.

6. Cut into squares to serve. In Cornwall it is topped with Cornish cream, a slightly sour thickened cream. If you like, have dairy sour cream mixed with chives, but it doesn't need the topping. Accompany with a green vegetable or a salad, and serve for lunch or supper.

note: In Cornwall the bacon is mixed in raw, but that is not the American taste, and the pie is more delicious and less fatty when the bacon is cooked first. If you prefer, you can cook it completely before mixing with the potatoes.

Sweet Potatoes with Ham and Chicken

preparation time: 15 minutes
cooking time: 1-1/2 to 2 hours
serves 8

2 pounds dry sweet potatoes
butter
1 pound baked country-cured ham
3 pounds chicken parts (legs, thighs, breasts)
fennel leaves
celery leaves
parsley sprigs
thyme
bay leaf
garlic (optional)
1/4 cup chopped parsley

This recipe is adapted from one in the Virginia Housewife (1856). In the style of old recipe books, it did not suggest any amounts.

1. Peel **potatoes** and cut them into thick lengthwise slices. **Butter** a 2-1/2-quart casserole and lay the potatoes in it.
2. Cut **ham** into thin slices and lay them over the potatoes. Remove skin and any excess fat from **chicken pieces** and place them on the ham.
3. Use as many or as few **herbs** as you like. Tie **fennel, celery** and **parsley leaves** together with the thyme if it is fresh. If thyme is dried, sprinkle it over the chicken. Put the **bay leaf** in the center of the casserole and add the herb bundle. Last, thread the peeled **garlic** clove, or cloves, on a wooden food pick or poultry pin, or tie with a thread (so it can easily be retrieved later) and add this as well. Pour in water to reach just below the top of the chicken.
4. Cover the casserole and bake in a 350°F. oven for 1-1/2 hours. Test the chicken and potatoes; if not tender, bake a little longer.
5. Discard the **garlic, bay leaf** and **herb bundle.** Transfer the meats and potatoes to a deep serving dish and keep warm. Return a few slices of potato to the casserole and mash them into the liquid to thicken it. (Or thicken it with beurre manié if you prefer.) Ladle the thickened broth over the meats and potatoes, and sprinkle with **parsley.**

variations: To make this easier to serve, use all one kind of chicken part (all legs, all breasts, etc.).
To make this more elegant, use 2 pounds chicken breasts, and skin and bone them. Cut the meat into slices a little thicker than the ham slices. Add 1 pound mushrooms, trimmed and sliced. Use less water if you use mushrooms, as they release a lot of liquid.

47

Al McClane's Potatoes Stuffed with Game Birds

preparation: 10 minutes, plus
time to dress birds
cooking time: about 1 hour
and 15 minutes
serves 6

6 baking potatoes, about 10 ounces each
6 small game birds (dove, railbird, snipe, woodcock), dressed
3 ounces butter, or more
salt and pepper
minced fresh herbs or crumbled dried herbs

If you live in an area where small game birds are plentiful, try this unusual method of preparation. Both birds and potatoes retain all their juices and flavor.

1. Cut raw **potatoes** lengthwise into halves and scoop out the pulp (use a melon-ball scoop), making a cavity large enough to hold a **bird,** but keeping the shell intact. Use scooped-out portions for another recipe. Preheat oven to 375°F.

2. Use the **breast meat** only (the legs hold only a sliver of meat). Stuff each bird into a **potato** and pack with **butter;** use more butter if necessary. Add **salt** and **pepper** to taste and **herbs** to taste. Press the potato halves together, enclosing the filling completely. Wrap each potato tightly with foil.

3. Bake potatoes in the oven, or, better, cook them on a charcoal fire until the potatoes are done when fork-tested. Serve in the foil. Each person will unwrap his own.

Spanish Potato Omelet (Tortilla)

preparation time: 5 minutes
cooking time: 15 minutes for
potato, 2 minutes per
omelet
serves 6

6 small waxy potatoes
1 onion, 3 ounces
5 tablespoons lard or olive oil
12 eggs
salt

1. Wash **potatoes.** Cover with boiling water and cook for 5 minutes. Drain. Peel and slice potatoes. Peel and chop **onion.**

2. Heat 2 tablespoons **lard** in a skillet and sauté potato slices, turning them often, for 5 minutes. Add **chopped onion** and sauté for 5 minutes longer. Remove from heat.

3. Beat the **eggs** well, but do not let them get foamy. Add 1 teaspoon **salt.**

4. Use a 6-inch omelet pan or skillet to make 6 individual omelets. Melt 1/2 tablespoon **lard** in the pan over brisk heat. Add one sixth of the **potato** and **onion mixture,** let it get hot, then ladle in one sixth of the **eggs.** Let the bottom set for a few seconds, then turn over the tortilla and cook the other side. If it is difficult to turn, place an oiled plate over the skillet, turn plate and skillet over, then slide tortilla into the pan, uncooked side down. Cook until delicately browned on the bottom, only a few seconds. Turn out onto a plate and keep hot until the other omelets are cooked.

5. Continue with the rest of the potatoes and eggs, using 1/2 tablespoon lard for each omelet.

variations: Add 1 pimiento, chopped, to the onion and potato mixture. Sprinkle 1 teaspoon grated cheese over each completed omelet. Mix chopped parsley with the eggs.
It may be easier for you to beat 2 eggs at a time; or beat 6 eggs at a time and make the omelet in a 10-inch skillet. However, individual omelets are more typical of Spanish service.

Irish Stew

preparation time: 15 minutes
cooking time: 3 hours
serves 6

3 pounds lamb for stew
3 pounds potatoes, 9 or 10
1 pound yellow onions
salt and pepper
1 teaspoon dried thyme
3 tablespoons chopped fresh parsley
3 tablespoons snipped fresh chives
1 bay leaf
4 cups lamb broth, or chicken stock, or water

1. Cut **lamb** from the bones and place bones at the bottom of a 3-quart stew kettle. (Or if you start the day before you can make lamb broth with these bones.) Cut the meat into 1-1/2-inch cubes; discard any excess fat.
2. Wash and peel all the **potatoes.** Set aside 6 potatoes and cut the rest of them and the **onions** into slices 1/8 to 1/4 inch thick. Put sliced potatoes on top of the bones in the bottom of the kettle.
3. Layer **lamb** and **onions** in the kettle, sprinkling each layer with a little **salt** and **pepper** and a little of the mixture of **thyme, parsley** and **chives.** Put the **bay leaf** in the middle. Put remaining **whole potatoes** on top.
4. Pour in the **broth,** stock or water. Add more if necessary; the liquid should come just below the top layer. Press a sheet of foil over the top, cover the kettle, and slowly bring to a boil. When steam escapes from the kettle, adjust heat to a gentle simmer and cook for 2-1/2 to 3 hours.
5. Spoon out a whole potato for each serving and the lamb and onions. The sliced potatoes at the bottom will have dissolved in the broth. Spoon a little of the thickened broth over each serving. Discard the bones.

Eliot Elisofon's Fish and Potato Bake

preparation time: 15 minutes
cooking time: about 1 hour
serves 6

2 pounds fillets of cod, haddock, or hake
1 pound yellow onions
1-1/2 ounces butter
salt and pepper
paprika
8 ounces sharp Cheddar cheese
2 to 3 cups fish stock
2 to 3 cups milk or light cream or a mixture
1-1/2 pounds potatoes

1. Rinse **fish,** pat dry, and cut into portions. Peel and slice **onions.** Use about 1/2 tablespoon **butter** to coat a 2-quart baking dish, wide rather than deep. Preheat oven to 375°F.

2. Arrange **onion slices** in an even layer in the buttered baking dish and place **fish** portions on top. Sprinkle fish with **salt** and **pepper** and a generous amount of **paprika.**

3. Slice **Cheddar** and arrange cheese slices on top of fish. Mix 2 cups each of **stock** and **milk** and pour it gently into the dish, until liquid reaches halfway up the fish layer. Use more liquid if necessary.

4. Wash and peel **potatoes.** Slice them, and arrange potatoes in an even layer to cover fish and cheese completely. Sprinkle potatoes with salt and paprika (no pepper, as pepper on top can become bitter). Dot the top with remaining **butter.**

5. Cover the dish with a sheet of foil. Bake in the preheated oven for about 50 minutes. Test the potatoes; if they are nearly tender, remove the foil and return the dish to the oven to brown on top; if not tender enough, bake covered for 10 to 15 minutes longer before browning the top.

Fisherman's Pie

preparation time: 15 minutes
cooking time: 40 minutes
serves 6

2 pounds haddock or halibut steaks
4 ounces butter
1-1/2 cups milk
1 bay leaf
1-1/2 pounds potatoes
salt
8 ounces onions
1/2 teaspoon dried tarragon
2 tablespoons flour
pepper
4 ounces Cheddar cheese

1. Rinse the **fish steaks** and pat dry. **Butter** a large skillet and a sheet of foil. Put fish steaks in the pan and pour in the **milk.** Put the **bay leaf** in the middle. Cover fish with foil, buttered side down, and make a few holes for steam to escape. Bring milk to a gentle simmer and poach the fish for 8 to 10 minutes, depending on thickness of steaks.

2. Pour off the **milk** and reserve it. Remove skin and bones from fish, and flake into large pieces.

3. Meanwhile, wash and peel **potatoes,** and cut into chunks. Cover with cold water, add 1 teaspoon **salt,** and bring to a simmer. Cook for 15 to 20 minutes, until potatoes are very tender. Lift them out to a clean saucepan or heatproof bowl. Save the cooking water. Set the pan of potatoes in a hot-water bath so they do not become cold.

4. While potatoes cook, peel and chop **onions** and sauté them in 1 ounce of the **butter** until translucent. Add to the fish, mix gently, and sprinkle with **tarragon.**

5. Butter a 6- to 8-cup casserole or deep pie dish. Melt 1 tablespoon **butter** in a saucepan and stir in the **flour.** When the roux is golden, pour in 1 cup of the **milk** reserved from poaching fish. Over low heat stir until thickened. Season with **salt** and **pepper** to taste. Mix into the **fish** and **onions** and spoon into the buttered casserole. Preheat oven to 400°F.

6. Beat remaining **butter** into the **potatoes** and mash them until smooth. Pour in any remaining **milk** reserved from fish poaching. If the potatoes are too stiff, beat in a little of the cooking water. Grate the **cheese** into the mashed potatoes and mix well.

7. Spoon **potatoes** over the fish, spreading them to the edge of the dish and covering the fish completely. Bake in the preheated oven for 20 minutes, or until potato topping is golden and the filling very hot.

variations: This can be made with leftover fish. Use 1-1/2 pounds boneless flaked fish. For a delicious different pie, use smoked haddock; omit salt in the recipe.

Other herbs can be used; or crush a few fennel seeds and add to the fish. Other cheeses can be used also; Parmesan is good, or for a delicate taste use Swiss Appenzeller. For a more buttery finish, dot the potatoes with about 1 ounce of butter.

Pennsylvania Dutch Potato Stuffing

preparation time: 20 minutes
cooking time: 20 minutes
makes about 2 quarts

2 pounds potatoes
salt
4 cups cubes of white bread
2 onions, 3 ounces each
4 celery ribs with leaves
2 ounces butter
1/4 cup chopped parsley
1 teaspoon poultry seasoning
1/4 teaspoon pepper
2 eggs

A similar potato stuffing is made in Nova Scotia near the Bay of Fundy, but there bread crumbs are used instead of cubes and the herb is sage.

1. Peel **potatoes,** cover with water, add 1 teaspoon **salt,** and cook until tender, about 20 minutes.
2. While potatoes are being cooked, toast the **bread cubes** in a 400°F. oven until crisp. Turn them over to crisp evenly.
3. Peel and chop **onions.** Wash and dry **celery** and cut into small pieces, including the leaves.
4. When **potatoes** are done, put them through a food mill into a large bowl, or mash them. Add the **butter** and mix in until melted. Add **parsley, poultry seasoning, onions, celery,** 1 teaspoon **salt,** or more if needed, and **pepper.**
5. Beat the **eggs** and mix in. Finally mix in the **bread cubes.** Use to stuff a 10-pound turkey or 2 large roasting chickens.

variations: Instead of toasting the bread cubes, some cooks soak them in cold water and squeeze dry. For a richer stuffing, add an extra egg. Chop 2 ounces salt pork, sauté until barely golden, and mix into the stuffing.

Rappie Pie

preparation time: 30 minutes on first day; 30 minutes on second day
cooking time: 4 hours for chicken and stock, 1-1/2 hours for pie
serves 8

1 large fowl, 5 to 6 pounds
2 bay leaves
2 tablespoons crumbled dried celery leaves
1-1/2 pounds onions
salt
4 pounds potatoes
1 teaspoon crumbled dried sage
1/2 teaspoon dried mustard
1/2 teaspoon lemon pepper
1 teaspoon celery salt
4 ounces butter
1 tablespoon oil
paprika
3 slices of bacon (optional)

This is one of Nova Scotia's great Acadian recipes. It takes time to prepare it, so you may wish to double everything and make a large casserole of this. It is a holiday dish, and can make a fine specialty for a buffet.

1. Start this a day ahead. Truss the **bird** and put it in a large heavy pot or kettle. Cover with water, bring to a boil, and let it boil for 5 minutes. Pour off the water, and wash the pot.
2. Return the **chicken** to the pot. Again cover with water, and add the **bay leaves, celery leaves, 1 onion,** peeled and cut up, and 2 teaspoons **salt.** Bring to a boil, then simmer for about 2 hours, until the bird is tender. You may find it helpful to turn the bird over halfway through cooking.
3. Remove chicken to a platter and let it cool until you can handle it. Leave the cooking liquid in the pot. Separate skin and bones, and return them to the pot. Cut the chicken into large chunks and refrigerate.
4. Bring the **cooking liquid** again to a boil and simmer for about 2 hours longer, until you have a flavorful stock. Ladle the stock through a colander into a large bowl or other pot. Discard all skin, bones and flavoring ingredients. Then ladle the strained stock through a fine strainer lined with cheesecloth. Cool the stock, then chill.
5. When **stock** is cold, lift off and discard the layer of fat on top. Measure about 4 cups stock for the pie. You will have more stock than you need for the pie. Refrigerate it; freeze it if you do not plan to use it within a week. You may also have more chicken than you need for the pie. That too can be frozen.
6. Next day, when you plan to serve the pie, wash and peel the **potatoes,**

and cut into small chunks. Drop the pieces into cold water until all are cut up. Have ready a large bowl. Set a colander in it and line the colander with a sheet of muslin (like a jelly bag) or a quadruple layer of cheesecloth.

7. Drop the **potato pieces,** a few handfuls at a time, into a food processor fitted with the steel blade. Grate the potatoes until there are no large lumps. The batch will look like a purée. Scrape this into the muslin or cheesecloth, and squeeze the bag to extract all the liquid from the potatoes. The liquid will be rose-colored, but in the bottom of the bowl there will be a thick layer of white starch. Do not discard the liquid. Turn the squeezed potatoes into a large enamelware or stainless-steel saucepan. Continue until all the potatoes have been grated and squeezed. (Originally potatoes were grated by hand. The food processor makes it much easier.)

8. Measure the liquid and starch squeezed from the grated potatoes. Discard it. Measure an equal measure of **chicken stock.** Slowly stir stock into the grated potatoes and set the pan over low heat. Stir in 1 teaspoon **salt,** the **sage, mustard, lemon pepper** and **celery salt.** Stir the potato mixture over low heat until it begins to feel stretchy (gluten is developing) and the mixture begins to pull away from the sides of the pan, like a dough. Be sure to stir so potatoes do not stick to the pan or burn on the bottom. Remove from heat.

9. Peel and chop remaining **onions.** Use about 1 ounce of the **butter** to coat the inside of a 2-quart baking dish. Melt 2 ounces of the butter in a large skillet and add the **oil.** Sauté chopped onions until just beginning to show some color. Mix in about 5 cups of the chicken pieces. Taste, and add more salt and pepper to your taste. Preheat oven to 400°F.

10. Spread about two thirds of the potatoes in the buttered baking dish, patting it around the bottom and sides in an even layer. Fill the potatoes with the **chicken** and **onions,** making the filling even. Spoon in the rest of the potatoes and pat out to cover the filling. Cut the rest of the butter into bits and dot over the top. Sprinkle with **paprika.**

11. Bake the pie in the preheated oven for about 1 hour. If you choose to use **bacon** (which is generally used in Nova Scotia), sauté the slices, keeping them as flat as possible, until about half cooked. Drain the slices, then place them in a single layer on top of the pie and continue to bake it for about 30 minutes longer, until bacon is crisp and top of pie is browned. If you omit the bacon, bake the pie for another 15 minutes, or until well browned on top.

12. To serve, cut into wedges if baked in a round casserole; cut into large squares if baked in a rectangular casserole. Accompany with a green vegetable, or a large salad.

Boxty

preparation time: 15 to 20 minutes
cooking time: 1 hour and 15 minutes
makes 12 pieces

2-1/2 pounds potatoes
4-1/2 ounces unsalted butter
1 pound all-purpose flour
1 teaspoon salt

Boxty, Irish potato bread, is said to be served on Hallowe'en; however, it seems to be at hand in most country kitchens all year long. It is never refrigerated, just stored in a drawer of the kitchen cupboard. It is like a potato shortbread or biscuit, heavier than regular bread.

1. Measure half of the **potatoes,** wash and peel them, cut into chunks, and cook them in unsalted water until tender. Drain, mix in 1/2 ounce of the **butter,** and mash well. Set aside to cool.

2. Wash and peel the rest of the **potatoes** and grate them raw. Use a food processor fitted with the steel blade if you have one. Scrape the grated potatoes into a muslin (like a jelly bag) or a quadruple layer of cheesecloth, and squeeze the bag over a bowl until all the liquid is extracted. Unwrap the grated potatoes and add them to the mashed potatoes. Let the liquid settle, then pour it off. Scrape the starch in the bottom of the bowl into the potatoes.

3. Mix **flour** and **salt** and sift the mixture into the potatoes. Mix well; it is useful to do this by hand for best texture; also one can find any large pieces of potato—these should be discarded or chopped up.

4. Melt the rest of the **butter** and slowly pour it into the mixture, stirring. Finally it will make a dough that can be kneaded for a few minutes. Preheat oven to 325°F.

5. Divide the dough into 3 portions and roll or pat each one into a circle about 6 inches across and 1 inch thick. With a wooden spoon make a cross on each; when baked the boxty can be broken into wedges (farls) along these divisions.

6. Bake on nonstick baking sheets for about 1 hour; breads should be crisp on the outside, but only lightly browned. When completely cold, wrap in wax paper and store in a cool place. If you refrigerate boxty, you will want to reheat it slightly before serving. Split the wedges and serve with butter.

variations: Make the entire boxty recipe, then add 1 teaspoon baking soda and enough milk to give the texture of a pancake batter. Cook on a lightly oiled griddle to make boxty pancakes. Serve with butter and sugar, or with bacon.

Potato Salad Niçoise

preparation time: 15 to 20
minutes
cooking time: 20 minutes
serves 6 to 8

2 pounds small waxy potatoes
1 garlic clove, peeled
2 shallots
3 tablespoons unsalted chicken stock
3 tablespoons dry white wine
2 ounces oil-packed anchovy fillets
1 head of soft-leaved garden lettuce
1/3 cup olive oil
2 tablespoons minced fresh parsley
1 tablespoon minced fresh basil
1/2 cup oil-cured black olives
12 cherry tomatoes, washed

An excellent summertime luncheon dish; also good for a buffet.

1. Scrub the **potatoes,** cover with boiling water, and bring again to the boil. Simmer for about 20 minutes, until they test done. Drain potatoes. Rub the **garlic** on the inside of a large mixing bowl; discard garlic. As soon as potatoes are cool enough to handle, but still quite warm, peel them and drop them into the mixing bowl.
2. When all **potatoes** are peeled, chop them in the bowl to random pieces, none larger than 1 inch. Peel and mince **shallots** and add to potatoes. Pour in **stock** and **wine,** gently mix, and set aside. Potatoes should absorb most of the stock and wine.
3. Drain **anchovy fillets** and cut into small bits. Wash **lettuce,** roll in a towel to dry, and arrange in a shallow round bowl.
4. Add **anchovies** and **olive oil** to potatoes and toss to mix. Arrange potato salad on the lettuce leaves, and sprinkle with minced **parsley** and **basil.** Around the edge arrange the **olives** and **tomatoes.**

Potato and Egg Salad

preparation time: 20 minutes
cooking time: 20 minutes
serves 6

2 pounds new potatoes (Red Bliss)
6 eggs, at room temperature
1 teaspoon salt
3 tablespoons white-wine vinegar
1/2 cup olive oil
8 ounces tender celery ribs with leaves
1 red onion, 4 ounces
1 green pepper
1/4 cup minced parsley
black pepper

1. Scrub the **potatoes,** cover with boiling water, and bring again to the boil. Simmer for 10 minutes, then gently slide the **eggs** into the water, one at a time, and let them hard-cook as the potatoes finish cooking. When potatoes are tender, empty the pan into the sink, cracking the eggs.

2. Rinse **potatoes** and **eggs** with room-temperature water. Potatoes should not be chilled. Peel them, and shell eggs. Cut both into thin round slices and drop into a pottery bowl. Gently mix them.

3. Dissolve the **salt** in the **vinegar,** then beat in the **oil.** Pour the dressing into the potatoes while they are still warm, and again mix everything gently.

4. Wash and dry **celery** and cut into thin crosswise slices. Peel the **onion** and cut into slices; break slices into rings. Wash and trim **pepper** and cut it across into thin rings.

5. Mix **celery, onion** and **parsley** with the **potatoes.** Sprinkle the salad with **black pepper.** Arrange **green pepper rings** around the edge of the bowl. Serve the salad at room temperature.

variations: Other vinegars, even lemon juice, can be used for the dressing. Olive oil tastes best, but other salad oils can be used.

German Potato Salad

preparation time: 15 minutes
cooking time: 30 minutes
serves 6

2 pounds small waxy potatoes
1/2 pound bacon (about 8 strips)
1 yellow onion, 4 ounces
1/4 cup cider vinegar
1/2 teaspoon salt
2 teaspoons sugar
2 teaspoons dry mustard
1 teaspoon caraway seeds
6 sour gherkins
garden lettuce
1 large pimiento

1. Scrub the **potatoes,** cover with boiling water, and bring again to the boil. Simmer for about 20 minutes, until they test done. Drain potatoes. As soon as they are cool enough to handle, but still quite warm, peel them and slice them into a heatproof pottery serving bowl.
2. While potatoes cook, place **bacon strips** in a single layer in a cold skillet (do them half at a time if they do not fit in the pan). Cook bacon over moderate heat until crisp. Transfer bacon to paper towels; when cool, crumble. Leave 1/4 cup of the bacon fat in the skillet; discard the rest.
3. Peel and chop **onion.** Reheat the fat in the skillet and sauté onion until golden and tender.
4. Pour **vinegar** into a small saucepan. Stir in **salt, sugar** and **mustard,** and heat until they are dissolved. Bruise **caraway seeds** in a mortar and add to the vinegar, then slowly pour the mixture into the skillet with the bacon fat and onion.
5. Let the mixture become very hot, then pour it into the **potatoes.** Use 2 wooden spoons or paddles to mix dressing and potatoes. Do not chill the salad.
6. At serving time, cut **gherkins** into slivers and mix into potatoes. Stuff **lettuce leaves** around the edge of the bowl. Cut **pimiento** into long thin strips and coil them around to make rosettes. Set them around the edge of the salad. Sprinkle the **bacon crumbles** all over the top.

Raw Potato Salad

preparation time: 15 minutes
cooking time: 10 minutes to
cook egg yolk
serves 6

1 head of romaine lettuce
1/2 red onion
salt
3 ripe tomatoes, each about 4 ounces
1 cup raw potato pieces
1 hard-cooked egg yolk
juice of 1 lemon
1/4 cup salad oil
1/4 cup creamed cottage cheese
pepper
chopped parsley

For this salad use the trimmings you have saved from making noisette or château potatoes. Store them, covered with water, in a plastic bowl with a cover. The water will discolor, but the potatoes will still be white and crisp.

1. Wash and trim **lettuce,** roll in a towel to dry, then shred into a salad bowl.
2. Peel and sliver the **onion,** sprinkle with **salt,** and let it rest at room temperature for 10 minutes, then rinse and dry very well. Put onion in a mixing bowl.
3. Blanch and peel **tomatoes.** Cut them into wedges and add them to the onion.
4. Drain **potato** pieces, rinse in fresh water, and pat dry. Cut them into chunks as evenly as possible. Add potatoes to the mixing bowl.
5. Press the **egg yolk** through a sieve into a small bowl. Add **lemon juice, oil** and **cottage cheese,** and blend with a whisk. Add **salt** and **pepper** to taste.
6. Pour dressing into the vegetables, toss gently to mix, and spoon the salad onto the shredded **romaine.** Sprinkle **parsley** over the top. The raw potatoes have a texture and taste not unlike water chestnuts.

Dorset Potato and Jam Tarts

preparation time: 20 minutes
cooking time: 40 minutes, plus
time to cook the potatoes
makes 10 to 12 tarts

1 recipe of short pastry (2 cups flour)
vegetable oil
2 ounces dried currants
1-1/2 ounces orange juice or Madeira wine
8 ounces butter
8 ounces sugar
2 eggs
3 cups (1 pound) plain mashed potatoes
10 to 12 teaspoons red jelly (currant, prune, strawberry, raspberry)

In Dorset these are called "cheesecakes." They don't taste like cheese, but no one can guess they are made of potatoes.

1. Make the **pastry,** roll it out, and cut out rounds to fit muffin tins or small tart tins, about 1/2-cup size. Brush the tins with **oil,** and fit the pastry into the tins.
2. Rinse the **currants,** then pour **orange juice** or **Madeira** over them and let them steep. Preheat oven to 400°F.
3. Cream the **butter,** beat in the **sugar** until it is no longer grainy, then mix in the **eggs.** Finally beat in the **mashed potatoes** until the mixture is smooth. Pour in **currants** and any liquid not absorbed.
4. Spoon 1 teaspoon of **jelly** into each pastry-lined tin. Divide the potato filling among them. (If there is extra filling, spoon it into custard cups.)
5. Bake the tarts in the 400°F. oven for 10 minutes, then reduce temperature to 350°F. and continue to bake for about 30 minutes longer. The tops should be golden brown, the edges brown, and the center puffed up.

Caramel Sweet Potatoes

preparation time: 15 minutes
cooking time: 1-1/2 hours
serves 6 to 8

2 pounds sweet potatoes
3 ounces butter
salt
1/2 cup pineapple or orange juice
grated rind of 1 lemon
1/2 cup firmly packed dark brown sugar
4 ounces shelled pecans, chopped

1. Bake the sweet **potatoes** following the basic recipe (see Index). When tender, peel them and put in a heavy bowl. Add half of the **butter** and a pinch of **salt** and mash until butter is melted. Then mix in the **fruit juice** and **lemon rind.** Reduce oven temperature to 350°F.

2. Melt the rest of the **butter** in a 6-cup top-of-stove casserole or iron skillet, and over low heat dissolve the **sugar** in it. When fully dissolved, continue to cook the syrup over low heat until it begins to color to caramel. Remove from heat.

3. Sprinkle **pecans** over the syrup, and spoon in the **potato mixture.** Smooth the top. Set the casserole or skillet in the oven and bake for about 30 minutes, until potatoes seem rather firm. The top will be dry and lightly browned.

4. Set a round serving platter over the pan. Hold platter and pan together (wearing potholder mitts, of course), and turn over. The potatoes will be sauced with golden caramel and sprinkled with nuts. Cut into wedges to serve. Serve with poultry, or as a dessert.

Sweet Potatoes in Oranges

preparation time: 30 minutes
cooking time: 1-1/4 hours
serves 6

7 large oranges with thick peel (Jaffa oranges are especially good)
6 sweet potatoes, each about 7 ounces
salt
3 ounces butter, softened
3 eggs, separated
1 teaspoon ground cinnamon
1/2 teaspoon ground cardamom
1/2 teaspoon grated nutmeg
2 tablespoons sugar

1. Grate the rind of **1 orange;** set aside on a sheet of wax paper. Use the rest of that orange for something else.
2. Cut a slice from the stem end of remaining **6 oranges,** and carefully scoop out the pulp, without damaging the shells. (This is the only difficult step.) Process or blend the orange pulp, and strain to get rid of the membranes. For this recipe, reserve **3/4 cup juice.** Store the rest in a covered jar in refrigerator, and save for another use.
3. Bake the **potatoes** following the basic recipe (see Index). When they are very tender, peel them and put through a food mill into a large bowl.
4. Add 1 teaspoon **salt** and the **butter,** and mix until butter is melted. Beat the reserved 3/4 cup **orange juice** and the **egg yolks** together. Stir in the **spices,** and beat the liquid into the potatoes until the mixture is homogenous. Preheat oven to 400°F.
5. Set the empty **orange shells** in a baking dish that will hold them upright, or hold them steady with a ring of aluminum foil around the base of each one. Spoon the **potato mixture** into the shells, making it level with the top. If there is more than enough, bake it in custard cups.
6. Beat the **egg whites** with a pinch of **salt** until foamy, then add the **sugar,** 1 teaspoon at a time, and continue to beat until meringue is glossy and stiff. Fold in the reserved **orange rind.**
7. Divide the **meringue** among the orange shells. Swirl it around with a spoon, or pipe it through a pastry bag, but be sure to spread it out to touch the shell all around. Bake in the preheated oven for 10 minutes, or until meringue is golden brown.

variation: To make a dessert, add 1/2 cup light brown sugar and 3 ounces medium-sweet sherry or brandy to the potatoes, and increase the sugar in the meringue to 3 tablespoons.

Index